PLACES TO WALK

GLORIOUS LIBERTY OF THE CHILDREN OF GOD

HENRY M. MORRIS III

INSTITUTE FOR
CREATION
RESEARCH

Dallas, Texas
ICR.org

Dr. Henry M. Morris III holds four earned degrees, including a D.Min. from Luther Rice Seminary and the Presidents and Key Executives MBA from Pepperdine University. A former college professor, administrator, business executive, and senior pastor, Dr. Morris is an articulate and passionate speaker frequently invited to address church congregations, college assemblies, and national conferences. The eldest son of ICR's founder, Dr. Morris has served for many years in conference and writing ministry. His love for the Word of God and passion for Christian maturity, coupled with God's gift of teaching, have given Dr. Morris a broad and effective ministry over the years. He has authored numerous articles and books, including *The Big Three: Major Events that Changed History Forever; Exploring the Evidence for Creation; 5 Reasons to Believe in Recent Creation; The Book of Beginnings; Pulling Down Strongholds: Achieving Spiritual Victory through Strategic Offense; A Firm Foundation: Devotional Insights to Help You Know, Believe, and Defend Truth; Six Days of Creation; Your Origins Matter;* and *Unlocking the Mysteries of Genesis.* He is also a contributor to *Guide to Creation Basics, Creation Basics & Beyond,* and *Guide to the Universe.*

PLACES TO WALK
GLORIOUS LIBERTY OF THE CHILDREN OF GOD

by Henry M. Morris III, D. Min.

First printing: November 2017

All Scripture quotations are from the New King James Version.

ISBN: 978-1-946246-05-9

Please visit our website for other books and resources: ICR.org

Printed in the United States of America.

TABLE OF CONTENTS

INTRODUCTION

"Thus says the LORD of hosts: 'If you will walk in My ways, and if you will keep My command, then you shall also judge My house, and likewise have charge of My courts; I will give you places to walk among these who stand here.'" (Zechariah 3:7)

—◊—

Zechariah the prophet lived at the same time as Haggai the prophet, Zerubbabel the governor, and Joshua the high priest. These served the small remnant that had come back to Jerusalem after the captivity in Babylon. The exciting visions God gave Zechariah look forward to the great conclusion of God's plan for this planet and His people.

In one vision given to Zechariah, Joshua the high priest is shown standing before the awesome throne in heaven. He is pictured as being clothed in filthy garments next to the angel who brought him. Satan was there with all his power, trying to resist everything Joshua was doing. Of course, the Lord was there too and rebuked Satan, calling Joshua "a brand plucked from the fire" (Zechariah 3:2).

What follows in the vision is a beautiful picture of what God does for us when we are twice-born. The Lord commands the angels to "take away the filthy garments" because, He says, "I have removed your iniquity from you, and I will clothe you with rich robes." The attendants quickly "put a clean turban on his head, and they put the clothes on him" (Zechariah 4-5).

When we are created by God as a "new man" while down here on Earth, the spirit is changed, along with a new heart and a new mind, but one day we will be clothed in fine linen that represents the righteousness of the saints (Revelation 19:8)—all given to us when we were made righteous by the marvelous grace of our Lord Jesus.

What Zechariah is shown about the Joshua of old is the vast promises of a close working relationship with the Creator Himself—judging His house, having charge of His courts, and being given "places to walk" among the great personages of the courts of heaven.

This little booklet will cover some of the highlights that describe what it means to be a twice-born child of God. At the most basic of biblical foundations, a Christian has been identified by the Creator as one He desires to spend eternity with!

YOUR PAST CONDITION

"And you He made alive, who were dead in trespasses and sins."
(Ephesians 2:1)

—∞—

Three concise descriptions are given in Scripture of how God sees all sinners prior to the creation of the second birth in us.

- We were dead in trespasses (activities) and sins (character, attitude, condition). The result was that we were unable to understand or seek God on our own (Romans 3:10-11). Nor are we able to know the things of God by our own intellectual prowess (1 Corinthians 2:14).

- We "walked according to the course of this world" (Ephesians 2:2), in bondage to the world (Galatians 4:3) and blinded by Satan (2 Corinthians 4:3-4).

- We are by "nature children of wrath" (Ephesians 2:3). Both our natural desires (Ephesians 5:5-6) and our willing unbelief (John 3:36) put us under an ever-increasing wrathful judgment of God (Romans 2:5-9).

The transformation performed by God on us can only be "His workmanship, created in Christ Jesus" (Ephesians 2:10). It involves God's rich mercy and great love (Ephesians 2:4) to make us alive when we were dead (see John 5:21-24; Romans 6:4-6, 9-11). That power raises and seats us with God in the heavens (Ephesians 2:6). That grace is effected through faith, and even "that not of yourselves; it is the gift of God, not of works, lest anyone should boast" (Ephesians 2:8-9).

Whatever being twice-born may ultimately involve, it assures us of permanent status as the chosen, holy ones of God (Romans 8:29-39), "that in the ages to come He might show the exceeding riches of His grace in His kindness toward us in Christ Jesus" (Ephesians 2:7).

Your Present Identity

"Now, therefore, you are no longer strangers and foreigners,
but fellow citizens with the saints and members
of the household of God." (Ephesians 2:19)

—⁂—

Prior to salvation, we are called "aliens...and strangers from the covenants of promise, having no hope and without God in the world" (Ephesians 2:12). But now we are a "new man" and part of the grand partnership that has been made possible between Jew and Gentile, old and new covenant saints, and the operative impact and purpose of the "household of God" (Ephesians 2:13, 19).

We are brought near and made one. The enemy has been abolished, with the "middle wall of separation" that was between us broken down (Ephesians 2:13-15), making us "one body" with common "access by one Spirit to the Father" (Ephesians 2:16-18).

Therefore, we are "fellow citizens...of the household of God" (see 1 Timothy 3:15), built on the foundation of the apostles and prophets, "fitted together," growing into a holy temple "for a dwelling place of God in the Spirit" (Ephesians 2:19-22), now displayed in a fellowship of past and present, bond and free, male and female...all new "partakers of His promise in Christ through the gospel" (Galatians 3:22-29; Ephesians 3:1-6).

Notice that "now the manifold wisdom of God might be made known by the church to the principalities and powers in the heavenly places" (Ephesians 3:10). This enormous impact is "according to the eternal purpose which He accomplished in Christ Jesus our Lord" (Ephesians 3:10-11).

God has designed His salvation for you in such a way that you cannot fail to achieve His plans for you! You should humbly thank Him for what He has accomplished in you through Jesus Christ.

YOUR NEW POSITION

"He chose us in Him before the foundation of the world,
that we should be holy and without blame before Him in love."
(Ephesians 1:4)

—∞—

The search for identity and meaning can drive one to great successes or tragic failures. However, for the Christian the question is answered through the Scriptures.

Chosen

You are selected as a favorite out of "many [who] are called" (Matthew 22:14) "out of the world" (John 15:19). What a privilege! You are God's choice to bear His name, represent His cause, and share His glory throughout eternity. In fact, you are "predestined [previous boundaries set]…to adoption as sons by Jesus Christ to Himself" (Ephesians 1:5). And "if children, then heirs—heirs of God and joint heirs with Christ" (Romans 8:17).

Accepted

Furthermore, you are "accepted in the Beloved" (Ephesians 1:6). That word "accepted" is a specialized form of the word most often translated "grace." You are "graced" by almighty God, who set absolute boundaries around your life and made you His child. You are purchased "through His blood" (Ephesians 1:7) "that He might redeem us from every lawless deed and purify for Himself His own special [precious] people, zealous for good works" (Titus 2:14).

Forgiven

Moreover, you are forgiven (Ephesians 1:7)! Your sins are covered (Psalm 32:1), cast behind God's back (Isaiah 38:17), removed "as far as the east is from the west" (Psalm 103:12), remembered no more (Jeremiah 31:34), as He has "cleanse[d] us from all unrighteousness" (1 John 1:9).

If you are God's child, you should have no identity crises. You are a chosen, predestined, accepted, redeemed, and forgiven holy one, predestined "to be conformed to the image of His Son" (Romans 8:29).

YOUR NEW NATURE

"...that we should be holy and without blame before Him in love."
(Ephesians 1:4)

—∞—

I n the grand purpose of our selection into God's family, two key words are used.

Holy

The word "holy" (Greek *hagios*) is the most frequently used descriptor about God's twice-born. It stresses dedication. A holy man or woman is distinctively God's, set apart for God's use, separated from the secular, and consecrated to God's service. All who are chosen are to be holy. The Colossians Christians were told to mortify the physical appetite, put off the sinful mental attitudes and habits, and "put on the new man...as the elect of God, holy and beloved" (Colossians 3:5-17). The focus is character.

Without Blame

"Without blame" refers to our reputation. This will only be finally realized in heaven (1 Corinthians 1:8), but there is a present responsibility to "present your bodies a living sacrifice....And do not be conformed to this world, but be transformed by the renewing of your mind" (Romans 12:1-2). The character of holiness is the cause for a lifestyle of blamelessness. We are to be the "children of God without fault in the midst of a crooked and perverse generation, among whom you shine as lights in the world" (Philippians 2:15).

This holy and blameless condition will result in "the praise of the glory of His grace" (Ephesians 1:6), where God will "gather together in one all things in Christ" (Ephesians 1:10). What a magnificent thought! The purpose for which we have been chosen, predestined, redeemed, and forgiven is to be holy in character and blameless in reputation so that when God gathers us all together in Christ, we will be the praise of the glorious grace of God!

YOUR NEW PURPOSE

"I, therefore, the prisoner of the Lord, beseech you to walk worthy of the calling with which you were called." (Ephesians 4:1)

—m—

We are called "out of darkness into His marvelous light" (1 Peter 2:9). Our calling is identified as heavenly (Hebrews 3:1) and upward (Philippians 3:14), and we are told that "the called" (Romans 1:6) are called "according to His purpose" (Romans 8:28). But we are also told to "be even more diligent to make [our] call and election sure" (2 Peter 1:10). There is much in Scripture about our calling, and although the calling is God's work and prerogative, we are expected to "add to [our] faith virtue, to virtue knowledge, to knowledge self-control, to self-control perseverance, to perseverance godliness, to godliness brotherly kindness, and to brotherly kindness love" (2 Peter 1:5-7).

We are "called to be saints" (Romans 1:7). That is, the purpose for which we have been invited by God to become one of His chosen is to be holy! Everything in our lifestyle should center on the fact that "we are His workmanship, created in Christ Jesus for good works" (Ephesians 2:10). Other aspects of our calling are the results of that holy character that should be the ever-controlling dominant factor in our lives.

The specifically cited traits in this context are attitudes of lowliness (see Philippians 2:1-3) and meekness (see Colossians 3:12-17), all the while "endeavoring to keep the unity of the Spirit" (Ephesians 4:3). A summary of this calling is found in Paul's closing comment to the Corinthian church: "Become complete. Be of good comfort, be of one mind, live in peace; and the God of love and peace will be with you" (2 Corinthians 13:11).

YOUR NEW AUTHORITY

"And Jesus came and spoke to them, saying, 'All authority has been given to Me in heaven and on earth. Go therefore and make disciples of all the nations, baptizing them in the name of the Father and of the Son and of the Holy Spirit.'" (Matthew 28:18-19)

—⟰—

Israel's high priest wore the inscription "Holiness to the LORD" to illustrate to all who obeyed God that they were "accepted before the LORD" (Exodus 28:36-38). High priest Joshua, as a type of all believers, was granted "places to walk" in the courts of God (Zechariah 3:7). Christ's disciples were commanded to ask the Father for whatsoever since they were chosen and ordained to "go and bear fruit" (John 15:16). We can "ask, and it will be given to you; seek, and you will find; knock, and it will be opened to you" (Matthew 7:7).

But there's more! Not only are we accepted, we are "sealed with that Holy Spirit of promise" (Ephesians 1:13). We are "establishe[d]... anointed...sealed" (2 Corinthians 1:21-22). We are confirmed in everything (1 Corinthians 1:4-8), consecrated and sanctified to serve (1 John 2:27), and given the Spirit as a "guarantee [down payment, deposit] of our inheritance" (Ephesians 1:14).

The Holy Spirit does His work through a threefold ministry in our lives. He will work on Christ's behalf, through our witness, to bring conviction to those not yet in Christ (John 16:7-11). He will also minister to us as the teacher of our spirit to guide us into all truth (John 14:17, 26; 15:26; 16:13). Furthermore, the wisdom, prudence, and knowledge of God are revealed to us through His work in us (1 Corinthians 2:9-10). All that is necessary for our "effective working" (Ephesians 3:7) is graced to us so that we can "work out [our] own salvation" (Philippians 2:12). We are "complete in Him" (Colossians 2:10).

YOUR NEW CAPABILITIES

"...that the God of our Lord Jesus Christ, the Father of glory, may give to you the spirit of wisdom and revelation in the knowledge of Him, the eyes of your understanding being enlightened."
(Ephesians 1:17-18)

—⋘—

The "spirit of wisdom" is applied to a wide variety of circumstances. It certainly includes leadership (Deuteronomy 34:9). But wisdom is also identified with the ability to make beautiful clothing (Exodus 28:3) and to engineer and invent complex equipment (Exodus 31:2-6). Daniel was said to have "an excellent spirit, knowledge, understanding, interpreting dreams, solving riddles, and explaining enigmas" (Daniel 5:11-12). We are even promised to be given wisdom that our "adversaries will not be able to contradict or resist" (Luke 21:15).

A "spirit of revelation" is also made available to us. This revelation (literally "to take off the cover") is not new doctrine or truth. Revelation is implemented by the Holy Spirit (1 Corinthians 2:10), having the source of His revelatory work from Jesus Christ on behalf of Christ (John 16:13-15).

The Greek language of the phrase "the eyes of [our] understanding being enlightened" (Ephesians 1:18) could be translated "the vision of your deep thought will be made to shine," or paraphrased in a more colloquial expression "the light comes on!" There are three specific enlightenments cited.

- The hope of our calling (see Romans 15:13-14)
- The riches of the glory of our inheritance (Romans 11:33-36)
- The exceeding greatness of His power exercised on our behalf (Ephesians 3:20; 6:10)

Each of those three are specifically designed by God to undergird our faith and embolden our confidence, even though we are "strangers and pilgrims on the earth" (Hebrews 11:13).

YOUR NEW EXPECTATIONS

"This I say...that you should no longer walk as the rest of the Gentiles walk." (Ephesians 4:17)

—⁓—

This succinct command is quickly followed by a sweeping description of the impotent mind of the Gentiles in contrast to the utterly changed condition of the believer. The Gentiles have a darkened perceptive ability, rendering them alienated because of the "ignorance that is in them" and an overall "blindness of their heart" that is the root cause of their inability to function, even to feel, in the same way as the children of God (Ephesians 4:18-19; compare Romans 1:21-32 and 2 Corinthians 4:3-4).

However, the saint of God is told to discard the "old man" and to "put on the new man" (Ephesians 4:20-24)—as though that simple picture of a powerful reality is adequate instruction to fulfill the earlier command. No longer is the child of God to be "corrupt" by the "deceitful lusts" of their old condition, but having "learned Christ" and "been taught by Him," the saint is to "be renewed in the spirit of [their] mind." A transformation is now possible through the new mental (intellectual, spiritual) abilities given to us by Christ (Romans 12:1-2; 1 Corinthians 2:16).

We are responsible to wear the new man like a body-enveloping cloak, created for us by the omniscient Creator "in true righteousness and holiness." Don't miss this! We have been given a specially created new man to wear (externally visible) that will show (exhibit, demonstrate, make clear) the spiritual difference between the Gentiles and the saints of God.

The 17 commands that follow in Ephesians 4:25–5:7 address every aspect of the Christian walk, all relating to a lifestyle of truth, giving specific contrast between the Gentile and the saint.

YOUR NEW RELATIONSHIPS

"...submitting to one another in the fear of God." (Ephesians 5:21)

—∽∽—

Our calling is to "walk worthy" (Ephesians 4:1).

Our behavior is changed by the "new man" (Ephesians 4:24).

Our wisdom is to "understand what the will of the Lord is" (Ephesians 5:17).

Our control is being "filled with the Spirit" (Ephesians 5:18).

Ephesians 5:22–6:9 presents a basic primer on human relationships in dynamics that impact most of our lives, our families, and our work. Our relationships are to be carried out by "submitting to one another in the fear of God." That key word *hupotasso* is instructive. It is composed of a preposition, "under," and a word that means "to arrange in order." Thus, "to arrange, under, in order."

In the home, the submission (order, arrangement) is compared to the Lord's house, the church. Wives are to be arranged under the husband (emphasis on authority) just as the church is under the authority of Jesus Christ (Ephesians 5:22-24). Husbands are to be under the responsibility of love (emphasis on sacrifice) just as Christ gave His life on behalf of, and for, the benefit of the church (Ephesians 5:25-33). Children are to be under the arranged order of their parents (emphasis on obedience) just as the Fifth Commandment requires for the protection and promotion of well-being and longevity (Ephesians 6:1-4).

In the workplace, those who serve are to serve as though they were serving the Lord, not men (Ephesians 6:5-8). Those who lead and own are to relate to their servants as though they were serving the servants, recognizing that one Master is over all (Ephesians 6:9). These instructions are really quite simple. Why do we complicate them?

THE POWER SOURCE

"And...the exceeding greatness of His power toward us who believe."
(Ephesians 1:19)

—∿∿—

The power of the triune Creator, as displayed in the resurrection of Christ, is directed toward us! We can be certain that we will never fully comprehend that, but the Scriptures provide several clear statements that will help us gain a small grasp on this magnificent resource.

- We receive power when the Holy Spirit indwells us (Acts 1:8). The Holy Spirit takes up residence in everyone who is twice-born (John 14:17) and is therefore readily accessible to all believers (Ephesians 3:20).

- We use the power of God every time we preach the gospel (Romans 1:16), whether to one person or to thousands (1 Corinthians 1:18).

- We learn of the power of God through "great and precious promises." Indeed, those promises involve "all things that pertain to life and godliness" (2 Peter 1:3-4).

- We see the results of the power of God in our lives when we are "strengthened with all might" so that we demonstrate "all patience and longsuffering with joy" (Colossians 1:11).

The Lord desires "that [we] may be filled with all the fullness of God" (Ephesians 3:19) and "strengthened with might through His Spirit in the inner man" (v. 16). The purpose of this empowering is to be "rooted and built up in Him and established in the faith" (Colossians 2:7), "able to comprehend...the width and length and depth and height—to know the love of Christ which passes knowledge" (Ephesians 3:18-19).

"Now to Him who is able to do exceeding abundantly above all that we ask or think, according to the power that works in us, to Him be glory in the church by Christ Jesus to all generations, forever and ever. Amen" (Ephesians 3:20-21).

THE POWER OF THE GOSPEL

*"For I am not ashamed of the gospel of Christ, for it is the power
of God to salvation for everyone who believes, for the Jew
first and also for the Greek." (Romans 1:16)*

—⁂—

This verse contains important information. We are told that God's power resides in the gospel—and indeed that the purpose of this power is the salvation of both Jew and Greek. This passage is intended to incorporate spreading the gospel to all humanity and is specifically stated by the Lord Jesus: "Go into all the world and preach the gospel to every creature" (Mark 16:15).

Evidently, the event that takes place when one is twice-born is nothing less than a supernatural creation by the Creator Himself (Ephesians 4:24)! There is no need for salesmanship or psychology or finesse or technique, the *dunamis* (power) of the Living God is transmitted, applied, and exercised as the gospel is spoken and a person listens.

- Ephesians 2:8—"For by grace you have been saved through faith, and that not of yourselves; it is the gift of God."

- Romans 10:17—"So then faith comes by hearing, and hearing by the word of God."

- John 6:63—"It is the Spirit who gives life; the flesh profits nothing. The words that I speak to you are spirit, and they are life."

- 1 Peter 1:23—"...having been born again, not of corruptible seed but incorruptible, through the word of God which lives and abides forever."

- 1 Corinthians 15:3-4—"...Christ died for our sins according to the Scriptures, and that He was buried, and that He rose again the third day according to the Scriptures."

To be successful (not to mention obedient) to the Lord's command, we must surely use the power of God that has been made available to us in the Scriptures!

THE POWER OF FORGIVENESS

"...to open their eyes, in order to turn them from darkness to light, and from the power of Satan to God, that they may receive forgiveness of sins." (Acts 26:18)

———

There is a point in our lives where the forgiveness of Christ was granted—even though He was "slain from the foundation of the world" (Revelation 13:8) and we were "predestined to be conformed to the image of His Son" (Romans 8:29).

Christ has subdued, cleansed, and forgotten our sins.

The triune Godhead paid the price to "subdue our iniquities" and metaphorically throw our sins "into the depths of the sea" (Micah 7:19). The Scriptures clearly tell us God blots out and forgets our sins (Isaiah 43:25; 44:22; Acts 3:19). God's forgiveness is an eternal act of forgetfulness as well as judicial payment and propitiation.

Christ has replaced our sins with His holiness.

A holy God cannot fellowship with an unholy being. "Therefore, if anyone is in Christ, he is a new creation; old things have passed away; behold, all things have become new." We must "become the righteousness of God in Him" (2 Corinthians 5:17, 21) so that He "might be just and the justifier of the one who has faith in Jesus" (Romans 3:26).

Christ has given us victory over sin.

Since all of the above is true and active in the life of every believer, there should be an obvious exhilaration that enables us to confidently stand against whatever "fiery darts" the Enemy may throw at us. "Sin shall not have dominion over you," we are told in Romans 6:14. Since sin has been dealt with on the cross, we should "reign in life" through Jesus Christ (Romans 5:17).

Do you rejoice in your forgiveness and therefore reign over sin in your life? God has made this possible.

THE POWER OF FAITH

"We also pray always for you that our God would count you worthy of this calling, and fulfill all the good pleasure of His goodness and the work of faith with power." (2 Thessalonians 1:11)

—⁓—

Whean God grants the gift of faith to enable us at the point of salvation (Ephesians 2:8), it is not a static power that merely resides in our minds but rather an empowerment that is expected to grow into a dynamic and demonstrable "divine nature" (2 Peter 1:4-9).

Faith preserves and protects us.

Jesus insists, "He who hears My word and believes in Him who sent Me has everlasting life, and shall not come into judgment, but has passed from death into life" (John 5:24). These words are precise. Once faith is exercised, an eternal transaction takes place wherein a person is passed from spiritual death to eternal life. This is an absolute change and eliminates the possibility of hell (John 10:28-29).

Faith is power for effective prayer.

The "mustard seed" promise in Matthew 17:20 does not refer to size or amount but to quality. The Greek comparative *hoce* translated "as" in that passage refers to the same kind of faith *as* the mustard seed. Just so, the promise of Matthew 7:7 (if you ask and seek, you will find) depends on our confidence (faith) in the heavenly Father.

Faith is the shield against the Enemy.

God's armor in Ephesians 6:10-18 lists "the shield of faith" that provides an ability "to quench all the fiery darts of the wicked one." That shield is defensive in the sense that it only provides protection when we use it to block the darts. The active use comes when we "resist the devil" (James 4:7) as we remain "steadfast in the faith" (1 Peter 5:9).

Do you use faith as God intended?

THE POWER OF THE COMFORTER

"It is to your advantage that I go away; for if I do not go away, the Helper will not come to you; but if I depart, I will send Him to you." (John 16:7)

—∿—

Declaring the gospel becomes a delightful use of the "power of God" (Romans 1:16), speaking God's words to a heart that has been prepared by the trifold ministry of the Holy Spirit, who will "convict the world" (John 16:8).

Conviction of Sin

"Of sin, because they do not believe in me" (John 16:9). All sin has been forgiven (1 John 2:2). The only sin that condemns is unbelief (John 3:19), or more accurately, conscious rebellion against the Holy Spirt as He "convinces" people of their need for salvation through Christ. Rejecting that message is blasphemy and unforgiveable (Matthew 12:31).

Conviction of Righteousness

"Of righteousness, because I go to My Father and you see Me no more" (John 16:20). When the Lord Jesus went up into heaven, there was "none righteous, no, not one" (Romans 3:10) visible on Earth. The Holy Spirit must convince people that righteousness *does* exist. Otherwise, they wouldn't understand why they need to be saved.

Conviction of Judgment

"Of judgment, because the ruler of this world is judged" (John 16:11). Some suggest the ruler is Satan, but there's no need to convince us that Lucifer needs to be condemned. But that the sinless Son of God was condemned on calvary for your sin and mine—that needs supernatural convincing!

Our powers of persuasion could never bring about a spiritual conviction of these matters in the heart of an ungodly and sinful person. However, the "One who comes alongside us" could indeed bring about such conviction. Our job is to speak the truth. The Holy Spirit's job is to be the supernatural Convictor and Persuader of that truth.

THE POWER OF GRACE

"...of which I became a minister according to the gift of the
grace of God given to me by the effective working of His power."
(Ephesians 3:7)

—⟶⟶—

In the New Testament, the words for gift and grace are closely related. *Charis* is usually translated "grace," and *charisma* is most often rendered "gift." The twice-born are to use their gifts with one another as "good stewards of the manifold grace of God" (1 Peter 4:10).

When God gifts us with faith so that we are saved by His grace (Ephesians 2:8), we are "created according to God, in true righteousness and holiness" (Ephesians 4:24). This "new man" is granted the potential to understand the "exceeding greatness of His power" (Ephesians 1:19) and to participate in the divine nature so we can escape the corruption pervading this godless world (2 Peter 1:4).

When we preach the gospel, we use "the power of God" that will result in the salvation of those who respond (Romans 1:16). Right after the Day of Pentecost, the apostles gave testimony of the resurrection of the Lord Jesus in a demonstration of that power so that "great grace was upon them all" (Acts 4:33). The message, the power, and the grace of God are inseparable.

When our lives radically change in response to the new man created in us by God, we do so by "the grace of our Lord," which is "exceeding abundant, with faith and love" (1 Timothy 1:14). When we access the strength to rise above infirmities or difficult circumstances, we experience the Lord's grace that is sufficient to deal with or overcome whatever may be hindering us (2 Corinthians 12:9).

When we "work out" the salvation God graced us with, we can be sure that God is working in us "both to will and to do for His good pleasure" (Philippians 2:12-13).

THE POWER OF A SOUND MIND

"For God has not given us a spirit of fear, but of power and of love and of a sound mind." (2 Timothy 1:7)

—✺—

The gift spoken of in the previous verse is based on a transfer of authority from God, and we are exhorted to "stir up" that gift (2 Timothy 1:6) because God did not give us a "spirit of fear." The word "fear" (*deilia*) stresses timidity or cowardice, not terror. The gift does not function well if we are too timid to use it.

The gift referred to is not power. That spiritual gift comes with *dunamis*—the innate ability to *do* the gift. Whatever the Holy Spirit has gifted us with upon our entrance into the Kingdom (1 Corinthians 12:11), that gift comes with the power necessary to implement and use that gift.

The gift also comes with love. Again, love is not the gift. It is only part of the fruit of the Holy Spirit that comes with the gift. Were it not for the reflection in us of the unilateral and sacrificial love of our Redeemer, these supernatural gifts could well be misused, distorted, and abused for personal glory. Diotrephes misused his gift, failing to use the spirit of love (3 John 1:9).

Sophronismos (sound mind) is a unique Greek word that is a combination of the verbs "to save" and "to control." Its basic meaning would be "safe control" or "wholesome control"—perhaps even "control that saves"—the perfect combination of abilities that empower the gift, the love that keeps the gift focused on others, and the "safety controls" to keep it from doing damage unwittingly.

"As each one has received a gift, minister it to one another, as good stewards of the manifold grace of God" (1 Peter 4:10).

THE POWER OF PATIENCE

*"But let patience have its perfect work, that you may be perfect
and complete, lacking nothing." (James 1:4)*

—⁂—

P atience (endurance) is part of the development that will produce
the experience that brings hope and assurance to those who are
the twice-born (Romans 5:3-5). Patience is a discipline—a work
that is necessary for our growth. Although such discipline never seems
pleasant at the time, it is administered by our loving heavenly Father,
who focuses His work on our spiritual maturity (Hebrews 12:5-8).

There are several key aspects identified in our text that promise
victory through the process of learning patience. Wisdom is granted
liberally as we ask for it during the tests that produce the "perfect
work" of patience. As we endure the tests that will come to those who
love the Lord, the endurance practiced will produce a "crown of life"
as an eternal testimony to our patience (James 1:1-12).

The principles for gaining patience during this life are outlined in
Psalm 37. First, trust in the Lord (Psalm 37:3) and follow His leading
in everything we do (Proverbs 3:5-10). Second, delight in (get excited
about) the Lord (Psalm 37:4)—amplified so often in Psalm 119 (vv.
16, 24, 35, 47, 70, 174). Then, commit your way to the Lord (Psalm
37:5), becoming such a part of Him that you are as a branch to the
vine (John 15:4-7).

Finally, rest (be still) in the Lord (Psalm 37:7) and wait on the
Lord (Psalm 37:34). These traits are not meant to be understood as
"hanging around." They describe the fully prepared servant, waiting
for his Master's orders to implement. The "profitable" servant (Luke
17:10) has learned what his Master wants and stands ready to respond
to the needs of the Kingdom.

Patience is never obtained through bored indifference.

THE POWER OF SPIRITUAL TOOLS

*"But to each one of us grace was given according
to the measure of Christ's gift." (Ephesians 4:7)*

—⚕—

The grace that is given (*charis*) is a distribution by the Holy Spirit of gifts (*charisma*) to every believer (1 Corinthians 12:4-11). Seventeen different gifts are listed in Romans 12:3-8, 1 Corinthians 12:4-10, and Ephesians 4:11. All of them are intended by the Holy Spirit to minister to the church and to enhance its unity (Romans 12:3; 1 Corinthians 12:12; Ephesians 4:12).

Three reasons are cited for these gifts.

The Perfecting of the Saints

This "perfecting" describes a process of making something useful or suitable that is not yet adequate. James and John mended their nets (Matthew 4:21). Paul prayed that he might supply that which was lacking (1 Thessalonians 3:10). The gifts of the Holy Spirit mend that which is lacking in the saints.

The Work of the Ministry

This is a joint effort of service (2 Corinthians 6:1) that recognizes the public visibility of that service (2 Corinthians 4:1-2) and steadfastly displays those gifts so that the "ministry may not blamed" (2 Corinthians 6:3).

The Edifying of the Body of Christ

The building process focuses the use of the gifts on the enrichment and betterment of the local assembly of believers (1 Corinthians 14:5, 12, 26).

The goal is to bring all the saints to a state of doctrinal unity (the faith) so that our maturity can be compared to "the fullness of Christ." (Ephesians 4:13). Eliminating susceptibility to "every wind of doctrine," growing up "in all things into Him," and building the body "joined and knit together by what every joint supplies, according to the effective working by which every part does its share, causes growth of the body for the edifying of itself in love" (Ephesians 4:14-16).

THE POWER TO EDIFY

"Therefore I write these things being absent, lest being present I should use sharpness, according to the authority which the Lord has given me for edification and not for destruction." *(2 Corinthians 13:10)*

—∞—

The older English word "edification" is used to render the Greek *oikodomos* that pictures the building of a house. We still use the word "edifice" to describe a structure of some importance. Paul specifically said he had the power to edify in the above text, and later called himself a "wise master builder," an *architekton*, a "first carpenter" who laid the foundation we would later build on (1 Corinthians 3:10).

When Jesus used *oikodomos* to depict those who might build their house on a rock (His Word) or the sand (ideas of men), He was painting a picture of how we should edify each other (Luke 6:48-49). The various leadership gifts are to be used to perfect the saints in the work of ministry (Ephesians 4:11-12), using the living stones that will build the "spiritual house" (1 Peter 2:5).

And like any good builder, the Christian carpenter has tools of the trade to assist the process. There are "things which make for peace" that must be employed (Romans 14:19). Most certainly love is a major tool (1 Corinthians 8:1), along with good communication that does not corrupt the building work (Ephesians 4:29).

Since "all things" are to be done so that the church is edified (1 Corinthians 14:26), it surely follows that "fables and endless genealogies, which cause disputes" are not helpful (1 Timothy 1:4). Effective communication demands that those we speak to understand what is said, therefore a mysterious tongue does not publicly edify like prophecy does (1 Corinthians 14:2-4).

An edified church walks "in the fear of the Lord and in the comfort of the Holy Spirit" (Acts 9:31).

THE POWER OF SPIRITUAL CONTROL

"Therefore do not be unwise, but understand what the will of
the Lord is. And do not be drunk with wine, in which is dissipation;
but be filled with the Spirit." (Ephesians 5:17-18)

—⟶⟶—

Two factors need to be identified with these verses. First, the preceding context confines the primary application to behavior, just as the following context relates the behavior to the fellowship of believers. Secondly, the imagery stresses control of that behavior by the Holy Spirit, contrasting drunken behavior with filled behavior.

The filling is not synonymous with the baptism of the Holy Spirit (1 Corinthians 12:12-14), since all twice-born are so baptized but not all are filled. Nor is it equal with or subsequent to speaking in tongues, since some specifically identified as being filled with the Holy Spirit (John the Baptist, Elizabeth, Jesus) never spoke in tongues. Some individuals (Paul, Peter, Stephen) were filled on different occasions. Apparently, the filling produces a temporary effect like alcohol does. The effect of the filling of the Holy Spirit enhances or encourages a God-like behavior in contrast to the Satan-like behavior stimulated by alcohol.

Some passages equate power with this filling (Acts 1:8; Romans 15:13; 1 Thessalonians 1:5), and others equate it to wisdom (Colossians 1:9-11; Philippians 1:9-11; Colossians 3:15-17). However, the immediate context lists four evidences of the Holy Spirit's control: songs of praise together, personal singing and private melody to God in our hearts, thanksgiving, and voluntary submission to one another in the Lord (Ephesians 5:19-21). Since the Holy Spirit distributes gifts to the saints (Ephesians 4:7-11) for the purpose of building the body of Christ (Ephesians 4:12-16), it stands to reason that the Holy Spirit's control would be designed to enhance and stimulate the ministry of believers to each other and their personal joy and awareness of the goodness of God.

THE CHILDREN OF LIGHT

*"You are all sons of light and sons of the day. We are not
of the night nor of darkness." (1 Thessalonians 5:5)*

—⁓—

"Walk as children of light," we are commanded in Ephesians 5:8. The title "children of light" is used only
three other times in the New Testament—once by the
Lord Jesus to contrast worldly wisdom with the ineffectual use of godly wisdom in the "least things" (Luke 16:8-10), once again to direct us
to "believe in the light" (John 12:36), and finally by Paul to encourage
us to "watch and be sober" (1 Thessalonians 5:5-6).

A light-like life, also called "the fruit of the Spirit," is expressed
in the character of goodness (Romans 15:14), righteousness (Romans
14:16-18), and truth (Ephesians 5:9; compare Galatians 5:22). In
fact, the transformation of our character by our conscious choice to
"present [our] bodies a living sacrifice, holy, acceptable to God" enables us to "prove what is that good and acceptable, and perfect will of
God" (Romans 12:1-2). An equation is clearly drawn between godly
behavior and godly wisdom.

It therefore follows that children of light should "have no fellowship with the unfruitful works of darkness" (Ephesians 5:11), taking
responsibility to "expose them" and recognizing that "it is shameful
even to speak of those things" (Ephesians 5:12). The "light" things
"make manifest" (present, display) that which is exposed, enabling
us to "walk circumspectly" (accurately, carefully), "not as fools but as
wise" (Ephesians 5:15). That wisdom is not the foolish wisdom of the
world (1 Corinthians 1:20) but the wisdom of God (1 Corinthians
2:7) that we might "know the things that have been freely given to us
by God" (1 Corinthians 2:12) and "understand what the will of the
Lord is" (Ephesians 5:17).

THE ARMOR OF TRUTH

"Therefore take up the whole armor of God, that you may be able to
withstand in the evil day, and having done all, to stand. Stand therefore,
having girded your waist with truth, having put on the breastplate of
righteousness." (Ephesians 6:13-14)

—⚒—

S cripture contains many military metaphors but none more fa-
mous than this passage on the armor of God. We are commanded to "put on the whole armor" so we can "stand" (be firm, well
established) against "the wiles of the devil" (Ephesians 6:11). Truth is
first on the list.

This girdle (lower body armor) was designed to protect from
wounds that would cause extreme pain and incapacity. Truth is our
protection against Satan's lie. "He is a liar," and "there is no truth in
him" (John 8:44). Satan uses this untruth to "deceive the whole world"
(Revelation 12:9). In fact, we are warned by Paul that the devil is able
to disguise himself and his followers as "ministers of righteousness"
(2 Corinthians 11:15). We can be spoiled by philosophy and other
false teachings (Colossians 2:8). We can be beguiled by good-sound-
ing words (Colossians 2:4). We can be tossed to and fro by crafty and
deceptive men (Ephesians 4:14). We can even depart from the faith
after listening to "deceiving spirits and doctrines of demons" (1 Timothy 4:1).

Our defense against these potential disasters is truth. Truth is the
essence of the strength of Jesus, who claimed to be truth personified
(John 14:6) as He fulfilled His mission as spokesman for the Father
(John 12:46-50). This truth is now verified by the Holy Spirit (John
16:13-15) and by the Word of God (John 17:17). We are to be doers
of the Word (James 1:22), to walk in the truth (3 John 1:3), and to let
our deeds be made manifest by doing truth (John 3:21).

THE ARMOR OF RIGHTEOUSNESS

"Therefore take up the whole armor of God...having put on the breast-plate of righteousness." (Ephesians 6:13-14)

The stand the Christian is expected to make "against principalities, against powers" of wickedness (Ephesians 6:12-13) is in large part made possible by the protection provided by the great breastplate of righteousness—the strong upper-body armor designed to ward off fatal blows of the enemy to our vital organs. Obviously, the strength of this armor can be none other than the spiritual "power of His might" (Ephesians 6:10). "The LORD [is] my Rock... my lovingkindness...my shield and the One in whom I take refuge" (Psalm 144:1-2).

This is none other than the gift of righteousness by which we reign in life (Romans 5:17), the new man of holiness (Ephesians 4:24), appropriated "through faith in Christ" (Philippians 3:9) by which we "might become the righteousness of God in Him" (2 Corinthians 5:21). "Thanks be to God for His indescribable gift" (2 Corinthians 9:15).

Yet, we are told we must take up and put on this armor (Ephesians 6:11-13). As soldiers engaged in active warfare, we are to "put on righteousness as a breastplate" (Isaiah 59:17), flee the desires of youth, and "pursue righteousness" (1 Timothy 6:11), separating ourselves from the unclean things and the unequal yoke of sin (2 Corinthians 6:14-18). We are to yield our bodies "as instruments [weapons] of righteousness to God" (Romans 6:13) and "awake to righteousness, and do not sin" (1 Corinthians 15:34).

This lifestyle of righteousness is the Christian's assurance that the Lord will bless and defend us in our battle "as with a shield" (Psalm 5:11-12). With God's righteousness, we can "go in the strength of the Lord GOD" (Psalm 71:16), and "in [His] righteousness [we] are exalted" (Psalm 89:16).

THE ARMOR OF SALVATION

"Therefore take up the whole armor of God...and take the helmet of salvation." (Ephesians 6:13, 17)

—⁊⊗—

I n the Christian soldier's armor, no piece is as indispensable as the helmet of salvation. Many soldiers have fought on after grievous and ultimately fatal wounds to their bodies, but a blow to the head (the mind) renders one either insensible, unconscious, or dead.

King David often described salvation in terms of military protection, as he did in his great song of praise written to commemorate the defeat of Saul (2 Samuel 22). It is a horn (mountain peak) from which to gain advantage over the enemy (v. 3) and a shield (protective line of troops) behind which we are safe (v. 36). It is a rock (natural fortress) from which one can safely attack (v. 47) and a tower, a place so safe it inspires boasting (v. 51).

Not only does this helmet protect us from the most damaging blows of the enemy, but it inspires us and emboldens us with confidence to take part in the battle. No soldier would ever fight without his helmet.

Yet, many religious leaders today encourage us to put on a helmet of "works of righteousness which we have done" (Titus 3:5), or to protect our minds with philosophy and the "tradition [teachings] of men" or the "basic principles [logical systems] of the world" (Colossians 2:8) rather than to place our faith in the risen Christ by embracing the grace of God's salvation. We become "wise for salvation" through a study of the Scriptures (2 Timothy 3:15) and thereby become able to "work out [our] own salvation" (Philippians 2:12) as the gospel, which is the "power of God to salvation" (Romans 1:16), makes it possible for God to work in us "both to will and to do for His good pleasure" (Philippians 2:13).

THE ARMOR OF FAITH

"Therefore take up the whole armor of God...above all, taking the shield of faith with which you will be able to quench all the fiery darts of the wicked one." (Ephesians 6:13, 16)

—⚜—

More than any other defensive piece of God's armor, this shield of faith is so important it is said to be "above all." Perhaps this is because it is to be used to "quench all the fiery darts of the wicked." These flaming arrows were designed to create fear in the soldier's heart and to set fires within the camp, thus driving soldiers away from their ranks and into the unprotected open. It worked, too, unless the shield was used.

Usually, the enemy would fire great volleys or salvos of arrows, thousands at a time, only seconds apart. Both the sights and sounds were terrifying. The sky was ablaze and the air alive with the hiss and sizzle of these awesome missiles. The most effective defense against this barrage was for all soldiers to form ranks together and raise their individual shields, joining them to form a roof over themselves and the camp.

When the arrows fell, they would clatter harmlessly on the firm roof. But let one soldier drop his shield or open a gap between his shield and those next to it until the fire storm was over, and a "fiery dart" would get through, setting fire to the clothing, equipment, or ground cover under the roof, which would quickly spread and destroy the "unity of the faith" (Ephesians 4:13), scattering the soldiers and giving an advantage—and perhaps victory—to the enemy.

These fiery darts are so effective they can be disguised as "ministers of righteousness" (2 Corinthians 11:15). But Satan flees if we "resist him, steadfast in the faith" (1 Peter 5:9) and above all take the shield of faith.

THE ARMOR OF PREPARATION

*"Therefore take up the whole armor of God...and having shod your feet
with the preparation of the gospel of peace." (Ephesians 6:13, 15)*

—∾∾—

I n the armor of God described in Ephesians 6, the shoes seem
somewhat mundane when contrasted to the more glamorous piec-
es. Yet, these shoes play a vital and indispensable part in the effective warfare of a Christian.

They are defined as "the preparation of the gospel of peace," with
the emphasis on preparation. Much could be said relative to the gospel (1 Corinthians 15:1-4), with its focus on the Lord Jesus' substitu-
tionary death (Isaiah 53:1-9), physical burial (Hebrews 2:14-15), and
bodily resurrection (Acts 2:29-36). The Bible identifies the creation
account as part of the gospel's message (Revelation 14:6-7), as well as
the promise of the eternal Kingdom (Revelation 11:15-18).

No gospel message would be clear without a presentation of the
true nature of sin and its awful consequences for the unbeliever (Romans 3:10-23; 2 Thessalonians 1:7-9) or without an understanding of
the anointed, incarnate Son of God (Isaiah 9:6; Acts 4:12).

The receiving of all these data requires preparation. Peter says that
we must be always ready to "give a defense [*apologia*] to everyone"
(1 Peter 3:15). Paul noted he was set "for the defense of the gospel"
(Philippians 1:17) and that we were to "know how [we] ought to
answer each one" (Colossians 4:6) and to participate with him in the
"confirmation of the gospel" (Philippians 1:7). This great work cannot
be carried out by the "wisdom of words" (1 Corinthians 1:17-18) or
in any way be misunderstood as "a different gospel" (Galatians 1:6-9).
Our feet must be shod with such solid preparation that we will not
suffer injury when our feet are dashed against a stone (Psalm 91:12)
and so that we can "run and not be weary...walk and not faint" (Isaiah
40:31).

THE ARMOR OF THE SCRIPTURES

"Therefore take up the whole armor of God…and the sword of the Spirit, which is the word of God." (Ephesians 6:13, 17)

—⁂—

I n the battle we wage against the principalities and powers of this world (Ephesians 6:12), only one attack weapon is given to us— "the word of God." This great sword, which is "living and powerful" (Hebrews 4:12), is what we live by (Luke 4:4), speak (Acts 4:31), preach (2 Timothy 4:2), teach, and glorify (Acts 13:48).

This weapon of our warfare (2 Corinthians 10:4-5) is not carnal (physical) but is mighty (*dunamis*: capable, able), with enough power to demolish the strongholds of the enemy and his most well-thought-out strategies (arguments), as well as every high (sophisticated, important, prestigious) thing that would exalt itself "against the knowledge of God." This weapon is so sharp (like a two-edged blade, Revelation 1:16) that it penetrates "even to the division of soul and spirit, and of joints and marrow, and is a discerner of the thoughts and intents of the heart" (Hebrews 4:12). In fact, the Word of God is capable of "bringing every thought into captivity to the obedience of Christ" (2 Corinthians 10:5).

With such a weapon, we can't lose, unless we keep it in the scabbard. It is worth noting that the Greek term used here for "word" is *rema*, used specifically of the spoken word. In our spiritual warfare, in which we must stand against the forces of evil, our weapon is the spoken Word of God. The great truths of God do no good sheathed between the covers of our Bibles. Faith, which is the channel through which God operates in the lives of people, "comes by hearing, and hearing by the word [*rema*] of God" (Romans 10:17). As Christians, we need to take out our swords, open our mouths, and preach the Word!

THE WHOLE COUNSEL OF GOD

"For I have not shunned to declare to you the whole counsel of God."
(Acts 20:27)

—⟋⟋⟍—

Sometimes it is good to step back and look at the "big picture"—the foundational perspective upon which the whole of Scripture is based. Four foundational passages in the New Testament provide pillars for the "whole counsel of God."

John 1:1-14

The Word (our Lord Jesus) was and is God.

The Word made everything that was made.

The Word was made flesh and dwelt among people.

Romans 11:36

For of Him and through Him and to Him are all things.

Colossians 1:16-20

By Him all heavenly and earthly powers were made.

By Him all things are saved from destruction.

By Him all things will be reconciled.

2 Peter 3:1-13

He destroyed the first world because of evil.

He will destroy this present universe by fire.

He will create a new heavens and new earth.

Sometimes we lose the enormity of the forest because we are looking too closely at each tree. Sometimes it is helpful to back away from the technical aspects of theology or denominational polity and review the whole counsel—the overall sovereign purpose of our Creator, Lord, and King.

"Remember the former things of old, for I am God, and there is no other; I am God, and there is none like Me, declaring the end from the beginning, and from ancient times things that are not yet done, saying, 'My counsel shall stand, and I will do all My pleasure'" (Isaiah 46:9-10).

SPIRITUAL WARNINGS

"Now this I say lest anyone should deceive you with persuasive words."
(Colossians 2:4)

—⟋⟍—

Anyone can beguile us with words that are designed to capture our reason. The unusual word chosen by the Holy Spirit to describe the process is *paralogizomai*. The basic meaning is "alongside of reason." It is used only one other time, in James 1:22: "But be doers of the word, and not hearers only, deceiving yourselves."

That self-deception is accomplished through "persuasive words" (*pithanologia*), used only here in Colossians. It couples the term for "reason" with "persuasion" and contains the foundation for the English word "analogy," a very similar process of using familiar words to transfer a known idea to something else. It is deception accomplished by transferring truth onto an untruth.

During His training of the disciples, Jesus often warned that it was possible for His followers to be deceived by those who would come and make attempts to claim some role with His authority. "For many will come in My name, saying, 'I am the Christ,' and will deceive many" (Matthew 24:5). "Then many false prophets will rise up and deceive many" (Matthew 24:11). "For false christs and false prophets will rise and show great signs and wonders to deceive, if possible, even the elect" (Matthew 24:24).

The stated purpose for gifted leaders in churches was to prevent the immaturity of disciples who would be "tossed to and fro and carried about with every wind of doctrine, by the trickery of men, in the cunning craftiness of deceitful plotting" (Ephesians 4:14). Although God has made provision for our stability in "wisdom and knowledge" (Colossians 2:2-3), we are warned that we can be beguiled by listening to the "persuasive words" of those who deny Christ.

THE NECESSARY LIGHT

"...to open their eyes, in order to turn them from darkness to light, and from the power of Satan to God, that they may receive forgiveness of sins and an inheritance among those who are sanctified by faith in Me." (Acts 26:18)

—⁂—

All humans understand the relationship between darkness and light. Those who love wickedness crave darkness to hide their deeds (John 3:19). Most of us feel better when the sun is shining and tend to be more susceptible to depression when clouds cover the sky.

Jesus insisted that He was the "light of the world" (John 8:12). Now in His gloried state, the Lord Jesus, our King of kings and Lord of lords, is described as "dwelling in unapproachable light" (1 Timothy 6:16). This is not mere metaphor. "God is light and in Him is no darkness at all" (1 John 1:5).

It is clear in the Scriptures that those who have not been twice-born must "come to the light" before they can receive the gift of eternal life (John 3:20). Indeed, the very process of coming is empowered by the drawing power of the Godhead Himself (John 6:44). No one who is "dead in trespasses and sins" (Ephesians 2:1) can come out of darkness into the light without the supernatural power of the Light Himself.

Once twice-born, once rescued from the darkness by the atoning sacrifice of the Lord Jesus and "birthed" from above by the power demonstrated in the resurrection of our Lord, we who are so redeemed become "sons of light" (1 Thessalonians 5:5). Thus empowered, we are to "walk in the light" (1 John 1:7) and have no fellowship with darkness (2 Corinthians 6:14). With the "armor of light" complete (Romans 13:12), we can openly let our "light so shine" (Matthew 5:16) that we become a "light of the world" (Matthew 5:14).

JANUARY 3

*If eternity is the plan, then it makes no sense to shrink your
living down to the needs and wants of this little moment.*

There is no doubt about it—the Bible is a big-picture book that calls us to big-picture living. It stretches the elasticity of your mind as it calls you to think about things before the world began and thousands of years into eternity. The Bible simply does not permit you to live for the moment. It doesn't give you room to shrink your thoughts, desires, words, and actions down to whatever spontaneous thought, emotion, or need grips you at any given time. In a moment, your thoughts can seem more important than they actually are. In a moment, your emotions can seem more reliable than they really are. In a moment, your needs can seem more essential than they truly are. We are meant to live lives that are connected to beginnings and to endings. And we are meant to live this way because all that we do is meant to have connection to the God of beginnings and endings, by whom and for whom we were created.

It's hard to live with eternity in view. Life does shrink to the moment again and again. There are moments when it seems that the most important thing in life is getting through this traffic, winning this argument, or satisfying this sexual desire. There are moments when our happiness and contentment shrink to getting those new shoes or to the steak that is just ten minutes away. There are moments when who we are, who God is, and where this whole thing is going shrink into the background of the thoughts, emotions, and needs of the moment. There are moments when we get lost in the middle of God's story. We lose our minds, we lose our sense of direction, and we lose our remembrance of him.

God reminds us that this is not all there is, that we were created and re-created in Christ Jesus for eternity. He reminds us not to live for the treasures of the moment: "Do not lay up for yourselves treasures on earth, where moth and rust destroy and where thieves break in and steal, but lay up for yourselves treasures in heaven" (Matt. 6:19–20).

Think about this: if God has already granted you a place in eternity, then he has also granted you all the grace you need along the way, or you'd never get there. There is grace for our fickle and easily distracted hearts. There is rescue for our self-absorption and lack of focus. The God of eternity grants you his eternal grace so that you can live with eternity in view.

For further study and encouragement: Luke 12:13–21

THE UNSHAKABLE FOUNDATIONS

*"For look! The wicked bend their bow, they make ready
their arrow on the string, that they may shoot secretly
at the upright in heart. If the foundations are destroyed,
what can the righteous do?" (Psalm 11:2-3)*

—∽∾—

Often we hear or feel the drumbeat of those who oppose the
work of God. Many would undermine our faith in God's
promises and try to shake our confidence in the authority of
His Word. David's short answers in this psalm are wonderful sources
of strength for us.

Trust in the Lord (Psalm 11:1).

He has not forsaken us (Psalm 9:10), and we are told to taste and
see that God is good (Psalm 34:8). Whatever happens, God knows
what we need, and He promises we will be taken care of (Psalm 37:3).
If we trust in Him and don't lean on our own wisdom, God promises
to direct our life decisions (Proverbs 3:5-6).

The Lord is on His throne (Psalm 11:4).

The picture of God's majesty can be easily lost in our sin-cursed
world. If we are not going to be overwhelmed by the wicked, we must
see God "high and lifted up" (Isaiah 6:1), surrounded by the great
host of heaven, recognizing that "heaven is My throne, and the earth
is My footstool" (Isaiah 66:1).

The Lord sees everything (Psalm 11:4).

His "eyes observe the nations" (Psalm 66:7), and He "knows the
thoughts of man" (Psalm 94:11). There is no place that will hide us
from His sight (Psalm 139:7-12).

The Lord judges everything (Psalm 11:5-6).

God loves justice (Psalm 37:28) and will finally come to judge
the earth (Psalm 96:13). "The LORD watches over the strangers; He
relieves the fatherless and widow; but the way of the wicked He turns
upside down. The LORD shall reign forever—your God, O Zion, to all
generations. Praise the LORD!" (Psalm 146:9-10).

HOUSEHOLD VESSELS

"But in a great house there are not only vessels of gold and silver,
but also of wood and clay, some for honor and some for dishonor."
(2 Timothy 2:20)

—∽∽—

The house referenced here by Paul to young Timothy is the "house of God, which is the church of the living God, the pillar and ground of the truth" (1 Timothy 3:15). In the Old Testament, the tabernacle and temple were the dwelling places of God and the centers of worship led by a high priest from the tribe of Levi.

Now, we are members of the Lord's house (Hebrews 3:6) and are like "living stones" that are being "built up a spiritual house" (1 Peter 2:5), led by Jesus, who is the "High Priest over the house of God" (Hebrews 10:21).

This "great house" has many vessels of different values. Some are honorable instruments (vessels of high value) that serve in the New Testament economy in some parallel function to that of the vessels of the inner court of the tabernacle and temple. Those instruments of gold, silver, and brass (Exodus 25; 2 Chronicles 4) each played a part in the liturgical worship, designed as part of the "tutor" to teach us about the law of God (Galatians 3:24). The more public and formal the use, the more valuable the vessel. The most valuable were set closest to the Holy of Holies.

There are also vessels of dishonor in the great house. The tabernacle and temple had earthen vessels for certain functions (Leviticus 14). These were expendable—necessary, perhaps, for some short-term need but not valuable. Since the church now functions as the "pillar and ground" of the truth, the "honorable" vessels are expected to purge themselves from that which is "dishonorable."

HUMANITY'S FIRST JOB

*"Then God blessed them, and God said to them, 'Be fruitful and
multiply; fill the earth and subdue it; have dominion over the
fish of the sea, over the birds of the air, and over every living
thing that moves on the earth.'" (Genesis 1:28)*

—⟁—

This verse is often called the dominion mandate and is repeated
again and amplified in Genesis 9:1-7. The purpose is clear:
accept the responsibility to bring into subjection all of Earth's
systems and creatures, effectively managing its resources, growing,
and expanding until the earth is filled with the fruits of that labor.

Man's First Job Description

When God made the garden "eastward in Eden" and placed Adam
there, Adam was to "tend and keep" that special and lavishly designed
estate (Genesis 2:8, 15) in the unique role as initial occupant but
more broadly as God's steward for Earth. Please notice that there were
no instructions on how to tend and keep, only the general orders from
the Owner to the steward.

Man's Implied Responsibility

Since there were no instructions about the functioning systems
of Earth, Adam must, therefore, first learn about the earth's systems
and processes (science), then organize and utilize the discoveries in
productive ways to help others and honor the Creator (technology).

The information about those practical inventions and products of
technology must then be accurately disseminated to everyone through
business, education, communication, transportation, etc.

And finally, both the information and inventions must be received so that the divine evaluation ("very good") is detailed in works
of music, art, and literature, glorifying and praising God for all He
had done in creating and making all things.

The ongoing responsibility is still in effect for us "as good stewards
of the manifold grace of God" (1 Peter 4:10).

UNDERSTANDING OWNERSHIP

*"The earth is the L*ORD*'s, and all its fullness, the world and
those who dwell therein." (Psalm 24:1)*

—∾∾—

The doctrine of creation is not merely a scientific debate. The opposite concepts of natural and evolutionary development versus the fiat creation of an omnipotent and omniscient transcendent Being impact every facet of our worldview. God owns the earth; He is the Creator (Genesis 1:1; Psalm 24:1-2; Revelation 4:11; and hundreds of other passages throughout the Bible).

Christians who revere the biblical revelation of God are not to be in conflict with this most basic of all doctrines.

- God owns the living creatures that inhabit the earth (Psalm 50:10).
- God owns the metals that establish monetary value on the earth (Haggai 2:8).
- God claims ownership over our bodies (1 Corinthians 6:19).
- God even has ownership of our very souls (Ezekiel 18:4).

Nothing is excluded from the sphere of His ownership and kingship (1 Chronicles 29:11-12; Isaiah 45:12; Colossians 1:16-17). We are to manage God's resources as stewards of the Owner.

Lucifer's grave error was that he thought he could become like the Owner, usurping all the rights and privileges of the Creator (Isaiah 14:12-14). Israel's error was similar; they were behaving as if their possessions were their property (Malachi 3:8-10). The prodigal son claimed for himself the right of ownership and treated the money as if it were his own (Luke 15:12-14). The unfaithful steward made no effort to be productive (Matthew 25:24-30).

We have been delegated authority over the creation itself (Genesis 1:28) and are required to be faithful with the "mysteries of God" (1 Corinthians 4:1-2), expected to administer "of the manifold grace of God" (1 Peter 4:10). May God preserve us from self-serving stewardship.

THE PASSION OF STEWARDSHIP

"And to love Him with all the heart, with all the understanding, with all the soul, and with all the strength, and to love one's neighbor as oneself, is more than all the whole burnt offerings and sacrifices." (Mark 12:33)

—⟋⟍—

It is interesting that our culture's regular diet of TV and Hollywood productions—grown far worse in many ways than in the radical '60s—is rarely scrutinized or subjected to criticism. Vitriolic attacks on religion in many media, however, have become both commonplace and increasingly intense. One wonders: Is there a reason for the passion?

God has a rather passionate view about His character and His unique authority in the universe.

"I am the LORD, and there is no other; there is no God besides Me. I will gird you, though you have not known Me, that they may know from the rising of the sun to its setting that there is none besides Me. I am the LORD, and there is no other" (Isaiah 45:5-6).

There are many details we do not and cannot know about the great work of God as Creator and on Calvary as Savior. However, it is clear that the same God who created the worlds (Hebrews 1:2) is the same One who died on the cross (John 1:1-3; Colossians 1:16-17).

It is nothing short of blasphemy to attribute the evolutionary story of the horrific, purposeless, waste-filled death of billions of living things evolving prior to the rebellion of Adam (Romans 5:12) to the omnipotent and omniscient God of love and grace. The naturalistic and evolutionary scheme of atheistic man is contradictory to God's written Word and to His revealed character. We must be absolutely committed to what God has said—whether the majority are passionately against it or not.

THE GOOD STEWARD

"But shun profane and idle babblings, for they will increase to more ungodliness." (2 Timothy 2:16)

—⁂—

A ll of us have seen ripples grow in concentric rings from a pebble plopped in a pond. Both the poet and the six o'clock newscaster love ripples. But they also make good illustrations of what atheistic and naturalistic science does to truth.

The Bible uses a number of illustrations about the importance of getting rid of the *source* of problems. The psalmist cries out for strength when he sees the enemies destroying the foundation (Psalm 11:3). Jesus warns about the leaven of false doctrine (Matthew 16:12), and the prophet notes that if the stump is left, the tree will grow again (Daniel 4:23, 26; contrast Luke 3:9). These illustrations warn us to focus on the *cause* of the error, not the *symptoms*.

It is tempting to go after the symptoms. The many effects of the dominant worldview (abortion, pornography, flagrant promiscuity, widespread STDs, easy divorce, political corruption, etc.) are very real and terribly destructive. But the core rationale in the educated Western world for all these anti-God, anti-righteous, anti-authority beliefs is atheistic, naturalistic science.

Ephesians 6:12 explains that the real battle is not "against flesh and blood, but against principalities, against powers, against the rulers of the darkness of this age, against spiritual hosts of wickedness in the heavenly places." A great part of biblical stewardship must be involved in direct opposition to these "rulers of the darkness."

Our world needs the evidence that will expose the atheism in naturalistic science. Christian leaders must not only be trained biblically but also in a defense of the faith "once for all delivered unto the saints" (Jude 1:3). That work is extensive, time-consuming, and expensive. Those called to so labor must have your prayer support. Please consider co-laboring with those of us engaged in this work.

Stewardship Conflicts

"You have made him to have dominion over the works of Your hands; you have put all things under his feet, all sheep and oxen—even the beasts of the field, the birds of the air, and the fish of the sea that pass through the paths of the seas." (Psalm 8:6-8)

—⟦⟧—

The initial commission to humans as the ruling stewards over Earth has never been withdrawn by the Creator. The implicit authorization for all the following basic human enterprises is in that dominion mandate (Genesis 1:28):

- Discovery of truth—science, research, exploration
- Application of truth—agriculture, engineering, medicine, technology, etc.
- Implementation of truth—commerce, transportation, government, etc.
- Interpretation of truth—fine arts, literature, theology
- Transmission of truth—education, communication, homemaking

When that authority was first delegated by the Creator, Earth was "very good" (Genesis 1:31). Implementing that command should have been a delight. However, Adam's failure in his first assignment created an ongoing conflict that now directly impacts humanity's efforts on every front.

The whole creation "groans" (Romans 8:22) as the very ground conflicts with the environment because of the Curse (Genesis 3:17-19, 23-24), which has led to the current state of affairs.

- Romans 5:12—sin and death as the condition of existence
- 1 Corinthians 2:14—ignorance of God's ideas, apart from God's revelation
- Ephesians 2:3—natural drive to serve ourselves, not God or others
- Ephesians 4:17-24—ability to obey comes only through God's new creation

STEWARDS OF MYSTERIES

"Let a man so consider us, as servants of Christ and stewards
of the mysteries of God." (1 Corinthians 4:1)

—⁂—

"Servants" is the translator's choice for *huperetes*, literally an under-oarsman, a term most frequently applied to officers of various kinds. The word rendered "steward" is *oikonomos*, an overseer or manager for any enterprise large enough to require "officers." The first term denotes authority under higher authority, the second indicates authority exercised within legal boundaries (Luke 16:1; Romans 16:23).

These titles certainly apply to Christian leaders, but they are also standards that all followers of Jesus Christ are to emulate. All of us are of the "household of God" (Ephesians 2:19), and we are each to serve one another as stewards of God's grace (1 Peter 4:10).

The limitation and exercise of authority demanded of the Corinthian readers were to "serve" and "steward" the mysteries (plural) of God. A practical dilemma for each Christian is to select where he or she will serve and give their time, talents, spiritual gifts, and resources. Of course, the primary place is the local church of which they are a member (Acts 16:5; 1 Corinthians 16:1).

Additionally, Christians are expected to give offerings (Acts 20:35; 24:17) to Kingdom needs and groups that are instructing and clarifying the mysteries of God. The ministry of the Institute for Creation Research deals with the "mystery" of those early Genesis accounts that are so critical and controversial in our day. We are stewarding the nature of the triunity of the Godhead (Colossians 1:12-16; 2:2) that displays the invisible character of God (Romans 1:20).

There are unique requirements today in our secular and scientific culture that necessitate a concentration of specially trained stewards who can refute the efforts of the many who deny the mysteries of God. We encourage your participation with those of us who accomplish this work.

STEWARDSHIP STRENGTH

"Then David said to the Philistine, 'You come to me with a sword, with a spear, and with a javelin. But I come to you in the name of the LORD of hosts, the God of the armies of Israel, whom you have defied.'"
(1 Samuel 17:45)

—⁓—

Our Lord Jesus taught that we could expect an ongoing condition of instability until He returns (Matthew 24:6). Every now and then, circumstances remind us that this world is not our home.

Psalm 2 is an important perspective for God's people to keep in mind. The physical circumstances often seem bleak, and the "bad guys" seem to have it their way much of the time (Psalm 73), but we are continually advised that their apparent success should not trouble us (Psalm 37:1; Proverbs 3:31-34; etc.), for "He who sits in the heavens shall laugh; the Lord shall hold them in derision" (Psalm 2:4).

"For though we walk in the flesh, we do not war according to the flesh. For the weapons of our warfare are not carnal but mighty in God for pulling down strongholds, casting down arguments and every high thing that exalts itself against the knowledge of God, bringing every thought into captivity to the obedience of Christ " (2 Corinthians 10:3-5).

The above passage is a source of encouragement for the ministry of the Institute for Creation Research. We see ourselves as fighting the "arguments" and the "strongholds" of those who set themselves against the authority of Scripture and the evidence of the Creator and His creation. The Western world has embraced the anti-God, anti-gospel message of evolutionary naturalism as its religion. ICR wages spiritual warfare against that terrible lie.

The battle is very specialized. God has brought dedicated "warriors" to ICR to engage the Enemy in his strongholds. We cannot fight without your financial support and intercessory prayer.

STEWARDSHIP INVESTMENT

"Render therefore to Caesar the things that are Caesar's,
and to God the things that are God's." (Matthew 22:21)

———ᴡᴡ———

The regular tax assessment by government has long been a disagreeable custom of civilization. Even our Lord Jesus found the subject important enough to comment on. All of us are aware of our responsibilities to "tribute" to those in authority over us.

Tribute money is *not* ours! In fact, the whole concept of tribute was initiated by God Himself in the tithe. One tenth of the "first fruits," God said, belonged to Him (Malachi 3:8-10; 1 Corinthians 16:2; etc.). The Creator God, of course, is the ultimate Owner of all things (Psalm 50:7-12; etc.). We are to be His stewards (Luke 12:42; 1 Corinthians 4:2; etc.) and have been delegated the responsibility to "do business" until He comes back (Luke 19:13; Matthew 25:14)

Here's the principle to remember: Although I have use of money, I also have certain obligations for that money. I may have freedom to do with the money whatever I wish, but I will suffer consequences if I choose to ignore the responsibilities to pay my "taxes to whom taxes are due" (Romans 13:7).

But we do have freedom to invest. God richly rewards those who make eternally wise investments with the "talents" and "minas" they receive from Him (Matthew 25; Luke 19). The tithe belongs to the Lord—and that should be deposited in the Bible-preaching churches in which we fellowship. But beyond that, our gifts and offerings may be deposited in Kingdom investments that will reap eternal dividends in the ages to come. What are you investing in?

The Institute for Creation Research is investing in work that confronts the godless worldview of the evolutionary naturalism that is robbing the minds and wrecking the faith of so many. Invest with us in this challenging work.

STEWARDSHIP AMONG THE CHURCHES

"He who has an ear, let him hear what the Spirit says to the churches."
(Revelation 2:29)

—∿∿—

Walking among the golden lampstands and speaking with the voice of the glorified King of kings, the Lord Jesus dictated seven poignant letters. Two letters contain praise and commendation. Two give grave warnings. Three are mixed.

Smyrna is faithful in the middle of terrible persecution and is promised a "crown of life" for its steadfast testimony (Revelation 2:8-11). Because of its attention to the Word, Philadelphia has an "open door" (Revelation 3:7-13). It serves the Kingdom with favor and with promise for victory.

Ephesus, although doctrinally sound, has a love that has grown cold and is in danger of losing its "lampstand"—the very church relationship that keeps it tied to service in the Kingdom (Revelation 2:1-7). Laodicea is oblivious to its danger of expulsion (Revelation 3:14-22). It is neither "cold nor hot" (neutral) and assumes that being successful and well thought of by the world is the church's goal.

These opposites reflect the reaction among today's evangelicals to the foundational issues of biblical creationism and the pervasive impact of the approach to biblical inerrancy. Some, like Smyrna, are standing firm in spite of denominational disdain, social ostracism, or limited resources. Larger "Philadelphian" churches are boldly ministering within their spheres of influence, heedless of the pressure to yield to the majority.

Sadly, many are similar to Ephesus and Laodicea. Like Ephesus, some are so concerned with technical nuances in doctrine that they have lost their love for the Word, lost souls, and the Kingdom. However, more are caught up in the neutrality of acceptance, like Laodicea, and are more concerned with "the praise of men" (John 12:43) than "sound doctrine" (2 Timothy 4:3).

The Institute for Creation Research is on the front lines of this critical battle for truth.

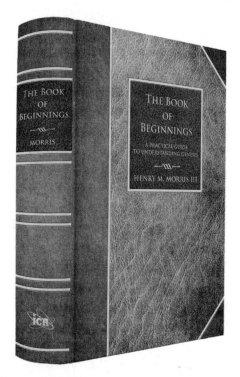